ORIGAMI
BOXES

DOVER PUBLICATIONS, INC., MINEOLA, NEW YORK

Bibliographical Note

Origami Boxes, first published by Dover Publications, Inc., in 2019, is a new English translation of the work originally published by NuiNui, Switzerland, in 2019.

Translation from the Italian: Martin Maguire

International Standard Book Number
ISBN-13: 978-0-486-84167-0
ISBN-10: 0-486-84167-7

Manufactured in China
84167701
www.doverpublications.com

2 4 6 8 10 9 7 5 3 1

2019

Text and diagrams

Vanda Battaglia

Riccardo Colletto

Rita Foelker

Francesco Decio

Francesco Mancini

Nick Robinson

Max Hulme

• •

Photographs
Dario Canova
Araldo De Luca
Céline Ribordy

Contents

Instructions

Choosing paper

Square-shaped sheets of paper are usually used when creating origami. Once you run out of the enclosed paper, you may purchase more in hobby shops or on the Internet.

- The best option would be purchasing large sheets of paper and then sizing them down to smaller square dimensions. This provides remarkable savings.
- Normally origami paper is two-toned: colored on one side and white on the other.
- You may use sheets of paper with different patterns and colors when creating the origami models in this book.
- Origami paper with a wide variety of patterns may be found for sale: choose the kind that is best suited to the origami model that you have chosen.
- We suggest trying your hand with less expensive paper before working on the final origami model with your nicest paper.

How to fold

- Arrange the sheet of paper on a hard, smooth surface, possibly on a well-illuminated table, and make sure you have enough space for comfortable elbow movement.
- Always remember that paper is a very sensitive kind of material and that once you make a fold, then it is practically impossible to eliminate all traces of that fold.
- Prepare every fold with extreme care: take all the time you need, concentrate on your work and make sure that the paper is perfectly arranged on the work surface.
- When you feel ready, take the lower edge of the paper and slowly lift it to the upper edge, always keeping the sheet of paper steady on the work surface with your other hand.
- When the two edges are perfectly aligned, start flattening the folds by delicately pressing them with a light movement in the direction of the fold.
- Finally complete the fold: in order to have a distinct and well-defined finish, press the edge with the back of your fingernail (usually using the thumb).
- Many prefer folding origami paper outward rather than inward, so that their hands do not get in the way.

Techniques

Name of the symbol	Aspects of the symbol	Application of the symbol	Result of the application
Valley fold			
Valley and unfold			
Mountain fold			
Mountain and unfold			
Repeat the crease once, twice, three times, etc.			

Name of the symbol	Aspects of the symbol	Application of the symbol	Result of the application
Fold to dotted line			
Inside reverse			
Hidden edges (to X-rays)			
Turn over			
Push, press, turn inside			

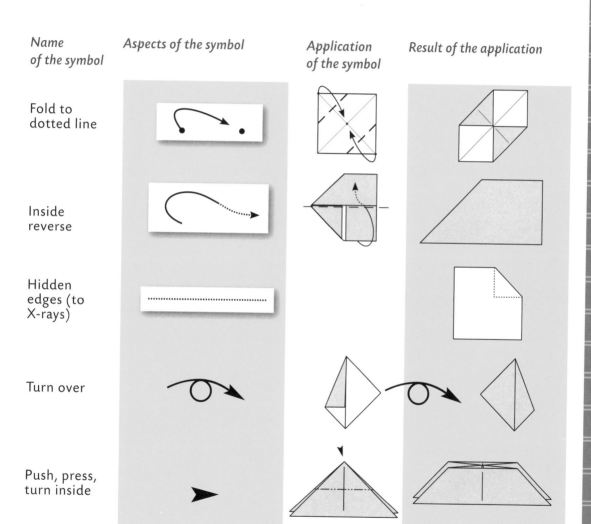

Name of the symbol	Aspects of the symbol	Application of the symbol	Result of the application

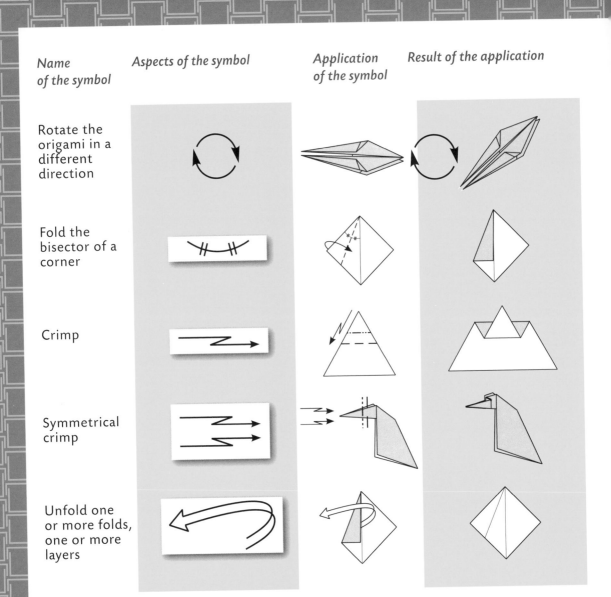

Rotate the origami in a different direction

Fold the bisector of a corner

Crimp

Symmetrical crimp

Unfold one or more folds, one or more layers

Name of the symbol	Aspects of the symbol	Application of the symbol	Result of the application
Enlarged origami			
Reduced origami			
Fold at 90°	90°	90°	
Bulge			
Transition to three-dimensional	3D	3D 90°	

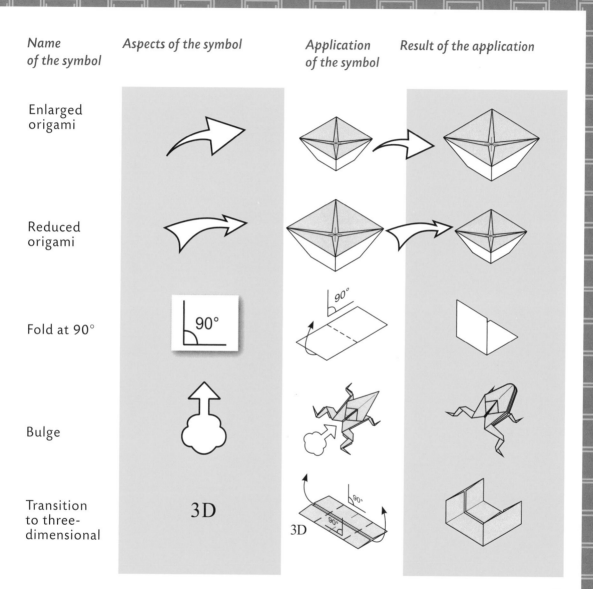

Tray for treats

Rita Foelker

This model evolved from the pencil holder. You can use it during parties to serve cupcakes, colorful candies, crackers, or tempting appetizers. And you'll see that your friends will be amazed by your origami skills!

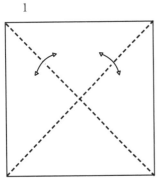

1. Fold and reopen along the diagonals.

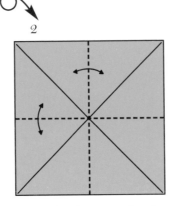

2. Turn the sheet over, bend and reopen along the medians.

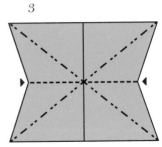

3. Use the existing folds to fold the paper into a triangular shape.

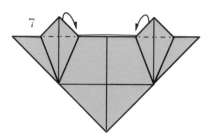

7. Insert the two triangles that pop up at the top inside the top layer of the model.

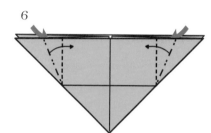

6. Open the tips you have just reopened by folding them as shown, so as to transform the valley fold into a mountain fold.

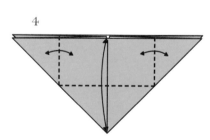

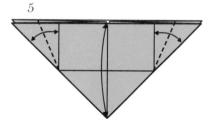

5. Fold the side tips until they reach the fold created in the previous step and reopen.

4. Fold the side tips toward the inside and reopen, then fold the lower tip upward and reopen.

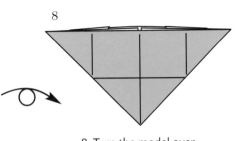

8. Turn the model over and repeat steps 4 to 7.

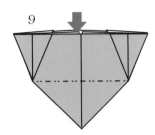

9. Open carefully, going over the folds well in order to obtain the three-dimensional model.

10. Your tray for treats is ready!

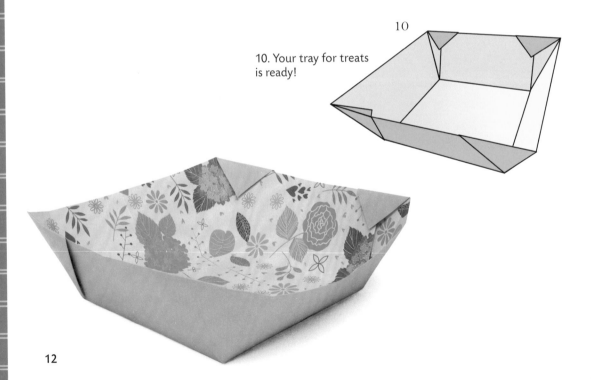

Wedding favor

Riccardo Colletto

The designer created this model for his wedding. Start with a square
sheet of paper of 15–20 centimeters (about 6–8 inches) on each side.
It is advisable to use paper that is not too thin, to allow the model to
be more stable.

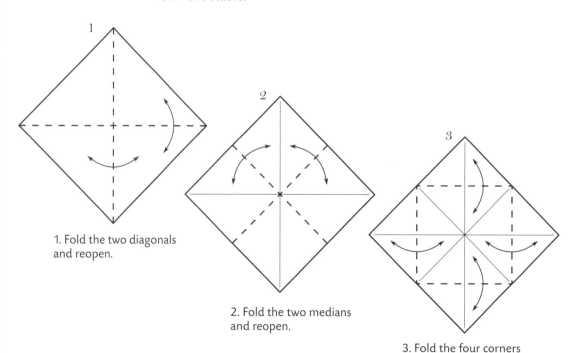

1. Fold the two diagonals
and reopen.

2. Fold the two medians
and reopen.

3. Fold the four corners
in the center and reopen.

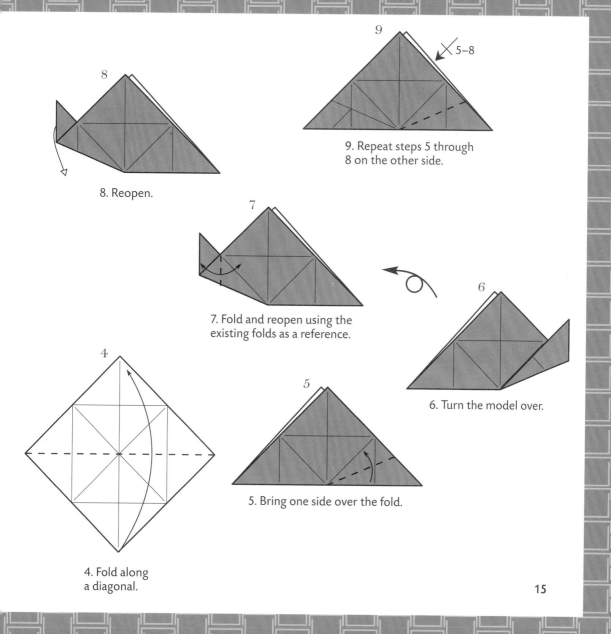

9. Repeat steps 5 through 8 on the other side.

8. Reopen.

7. Fold and reopen using the existing folds as a reference.

6. Turn the model over.

5. Bring one side over the fold.

4. Fold along a diagonal.

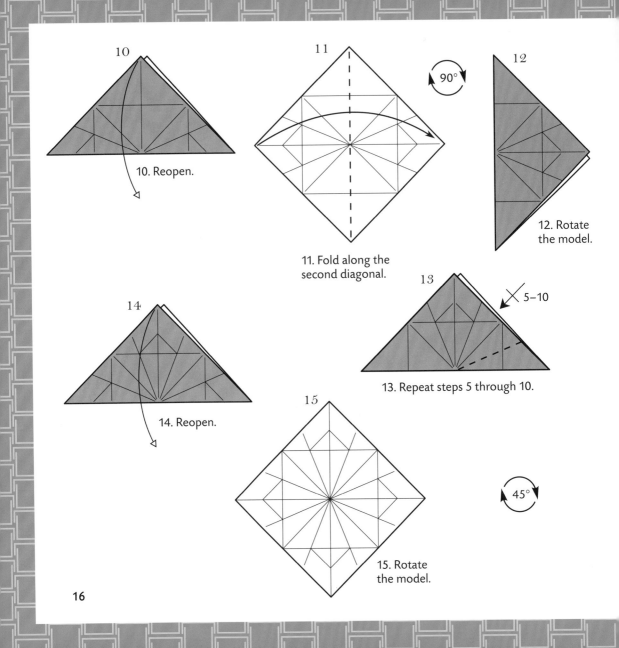

10

10. Reopen.

11

90°

11. Fold along the
second diagonal.

12

12. Rotate
the model.

13

5–10

13. Repeat steps 5 through 10.

14

14. Reopen.

15

45°

15. Rotate
the model.

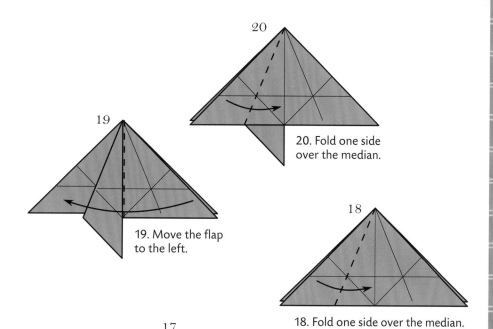

20. Fold one side over the median.

19. Move the flap to the left.

18. Fold one side over the median.

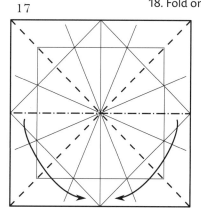

17. Form a triangular base.

16. Extend the existing folds and reopen them.

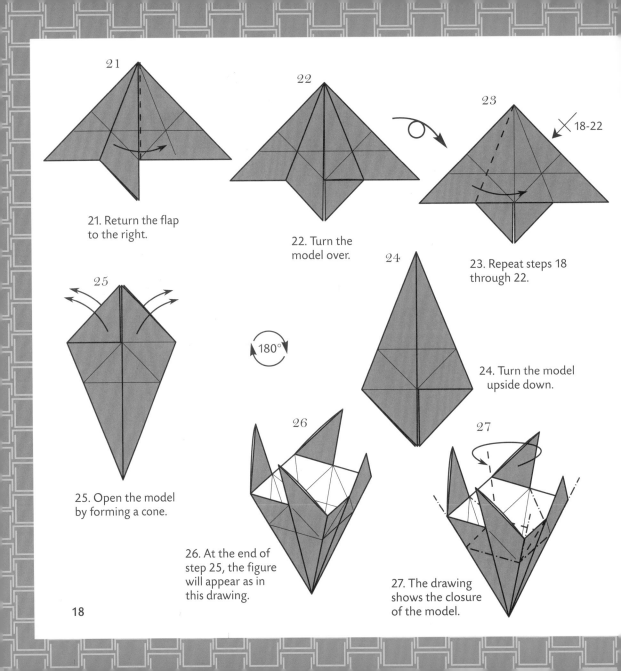

21. Return the flap to the right.

22. Turn the model over.

23. Repeat steps 18 through 22.

18-22

24. Turn the model upside down.

180°

25. Open the model by forming a cone.

26. At the end of step 25, the figure will appear as in this drawing.

27. The drawing shows the closure of the model.

18

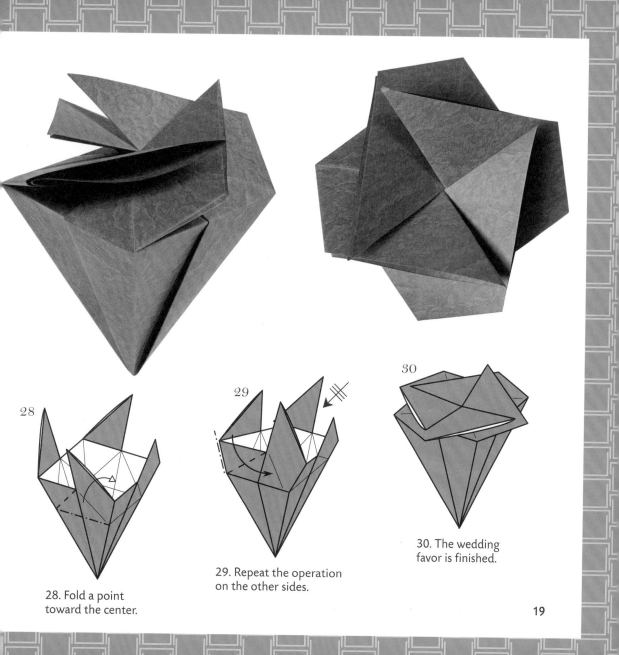

28. Fold a point toward the center.

29. Repeat the operation on the other sides.

30. The wedding favor is finished.

Flat box

Francesco Decio and Vanda Battaglia

This box is a real classic origami creation, as well as a very practical object and one of the most common models because of its wide range of uses. The one proposed here, easy to make, is a truly original container because it can be closed or opened with a small, simple gesture. You can easily customize it with a careful choice of paper, playing with colors and patterns.

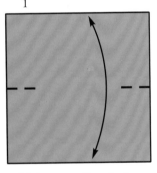

1. Make two valley pinches on the colored side.

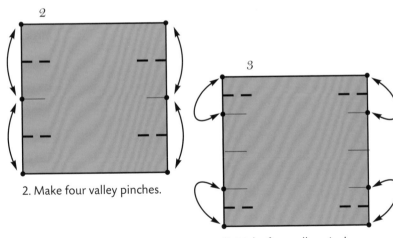

2. Make four valley pinches.

3. Make four valley pinches.

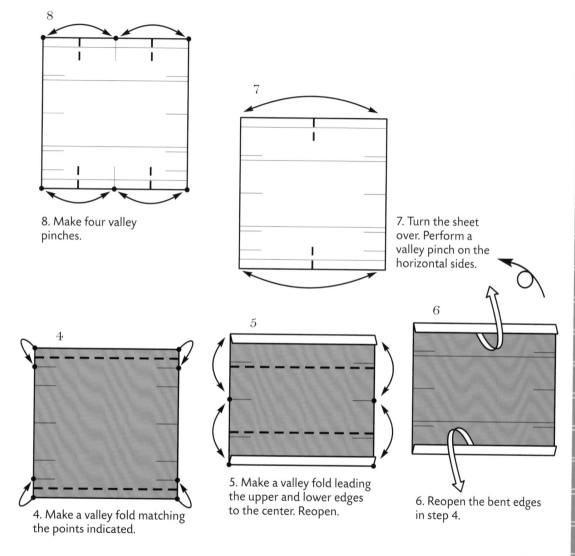

8. Make four valley pinches.

7. Turn the sheet over. Perform a valley pinch on the horizontal sides.

5. Make a valley fold leading the upper and lower edges to the center. Reopen.

6. Reopen the bent edges in step 4.

4. Make a valley fold matching the points indicated.

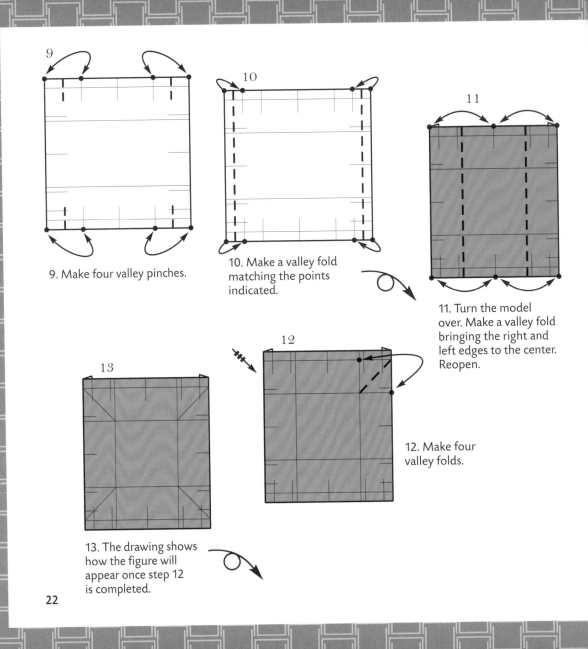

9. Make four valley pinches.

10. Make a valley fold matching the points indicated.

11. Turn the model over. Make a valley fold bringing the right and left edges to the center. Reopen.

12. Make four valley folds.

13. The drawing shows how the figure will appear once step 12 is completed.

22

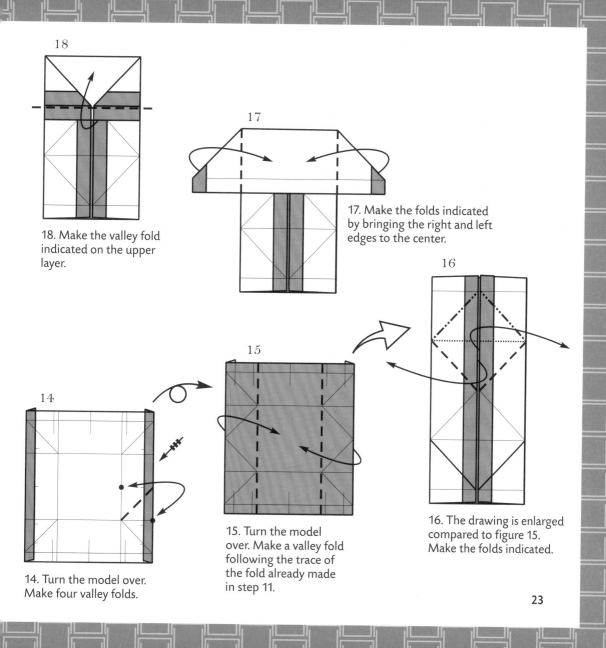

18. Make the valley fold indicated on the upper layer.

17. Make the folds indicated by bringing the right and left edges to the center.

16. The drawing is enlarged compared to figure 15. Make the folds indicated.

15. Turn the model over. Make a valley fold following the trace of the fold already made in step 11.

14. Turn the model over. Make four valley folds.

19

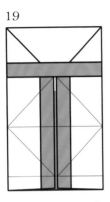

19. The drawing shows how the figure will appear once step 18 is completed.

16-17-18

20

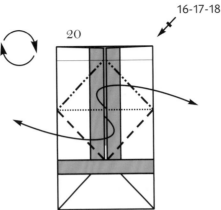

20. Rotate the model 180° and repeat the folds performed in steps 16, 17, and 18.

21 3D

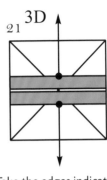

21. Take the edges indicated by the black dots and pull in opposite directions. The model will now go into 3D.

22

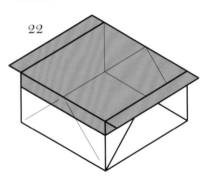

22. The drawing shows how the figure will appear once step 21 is completed.

23

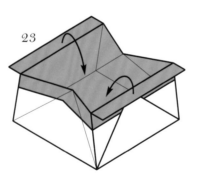

23. Push down the edges held in step 21 to flatten the box again.

24

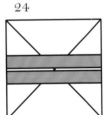

24. The box, once again flattened, is complete.

Arlington box

Nick Robinson

This design is named after the sleepy village where my good friend
Joan Homewood lives. I created the model while staying there.

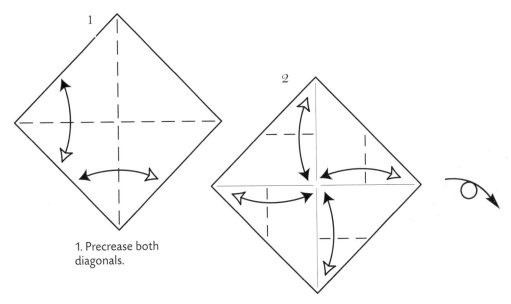

1. Precrease both
diagonals.

2. Fold each corner to the center,
crease the indicated areas only,
then unfold. Turn the paper over.

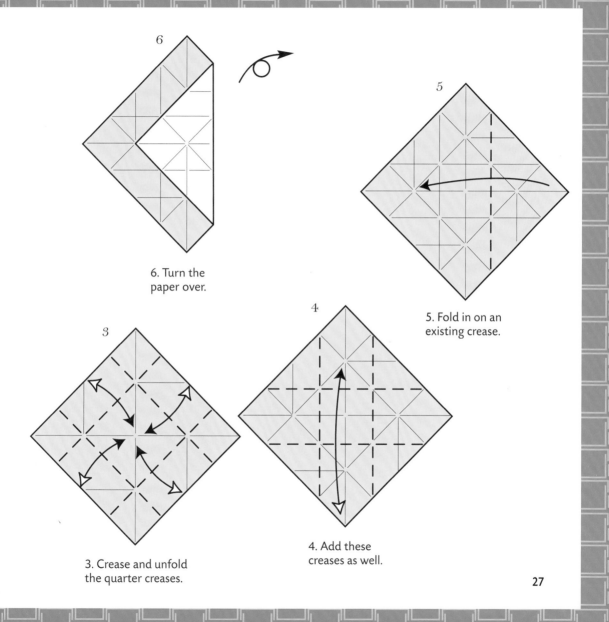

6. Turn the paper over.

5. Fold in on an existing crease.

3. Crease and unfold the quarter creases.

4. Add these creases as well.

27

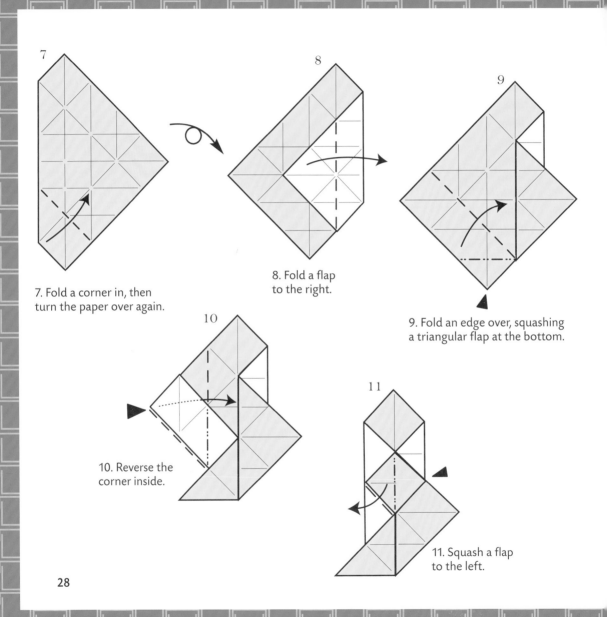

7. Fold a corner in, then turn the paper over again.

8. Fold a flap to the right.

9. Fold an edge over, squashing a triangular flap at the bottom.

10. Reverse the corner inside.

11. Squash a flap to the left.

Although boxes are always fun to fold, the end result of this model isn't the main point. Many creators obsess about how accurate the final result is. To my mind, origami is a journey as well as a destination. The sequence has been carefully designed to provide an interesting and flowing journey. Your results may vary!

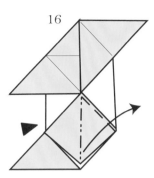

16. Repeat at the bottom.

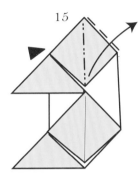

15 Open out a flap at the top.

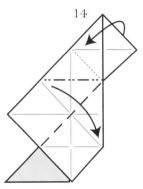

14. Fold the lower white flap over, making a valley fold on the hidden (dotted) crease at the same time.

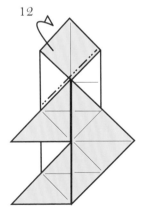

12. Fold the upper flap behind.

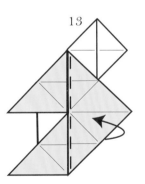

13. Fold over a triangular flap.

29

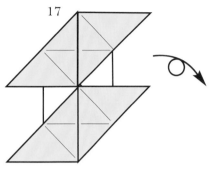

17. Here's the result. Turn the paper over.

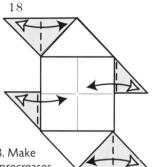

18. Make 4 precreases.

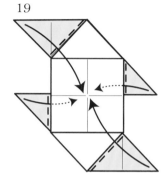

19. Tuck the side flaps under a layer. Fold the upper and lower flaps inward.

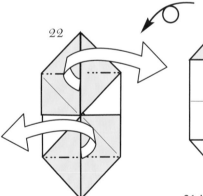

22. Open the model into 3D and reinforce the creases along the edges.

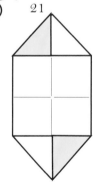

21. Here's the result. Turn the model over.

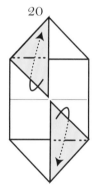

20. Tuck two flaps behind into pockets.

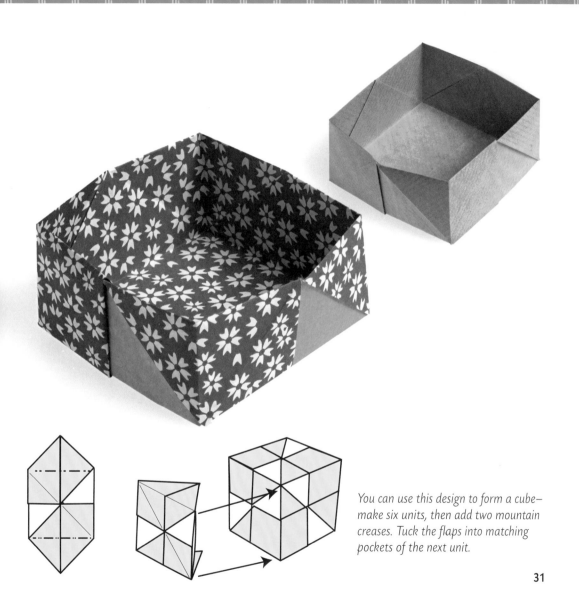

You can use this design to form a cube—make six units, then add two mountain creases. Tuck the flaps into matching pockets of the next unit.

Ancient Japanese box

Francesco Decio and Vanda Battaglia

Keeping your belongings tidy is important: this simple box, one of the oldest traditional models, maintains the charm linked to its special shape and is suitable for holding the most varied objects. You are free to make it with cardstock in solid color tones or in tones in stark contrast but can also use sheets with the varied patterns.

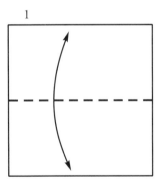

1. The first steps are necessary to get the starting shape, which in this case it is not a square, but a rectangle with proportions of about 3:2. Fold and reopen the horizontal median of a square.

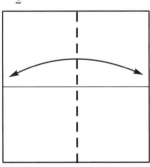

2. Fold and reopen the vertical median.

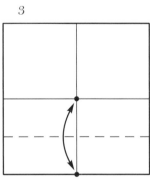

3. Bring the lower side to the center, then fold and reopen.

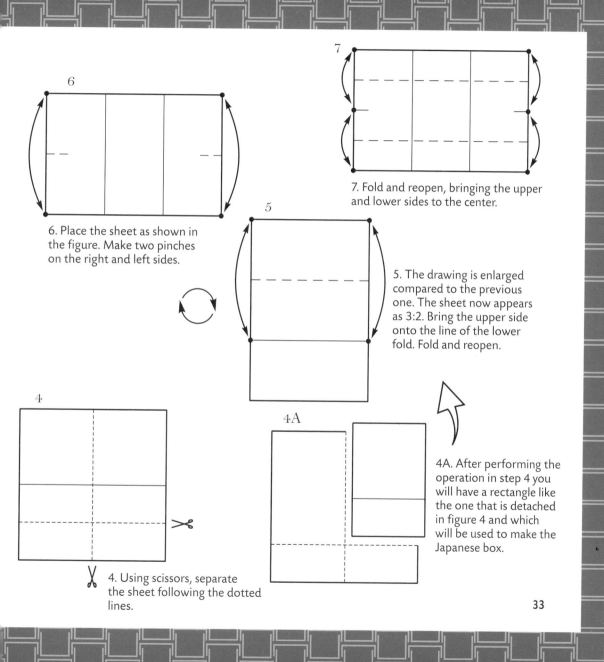

6. Place the sheet as shown in the figure. Make two pinches on the right and left sides.

7. Fold and reopen, bringing the upper and lower sides to the center.

5. The drawing is enlarged compared to the previous one. The sheet now appears as 3:2. Bring the upper side onto the line of the lower fold. Fold and reopen.

4A. After performing the operation in step 4 you will have a rectangle like the one that is detached in figure 4 and which will be used to make the Japanese box.

4. Using scissors, separate the sheet following the dotted lines.

33

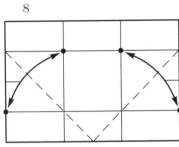

8. Make two 45° folds, bringing the points indicated to meet and then reopen.

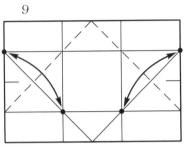

9. Perform two more 45° folds, bringing the points indicated to meet and then reopen.

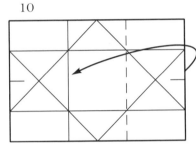

10. Fold the right edge following the existing fold.

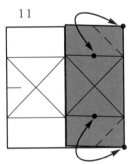

11. Make two 45° folds, bringing the points indicated to meet and then reopen.

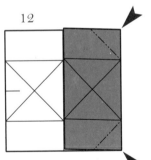

12. Make two inside reverses on the angles indicated.

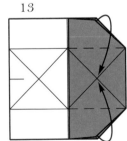

13. Lift and move only the upper edges to the center.

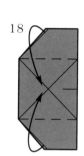

18. Lift and carry to the center only the upper edges.

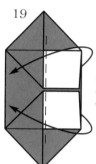

19. The drawing is enlarged compared to the previous one. Move the indicated white layer to the left.

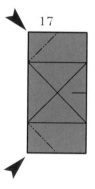

17. Make two inside reverses on the angles indicated.

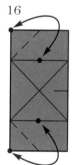

16. Make two 45° folds, bringing the points indicated to meet and then reopen.

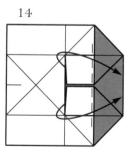

14. Fold the white layer to the right as shown in figure 14.

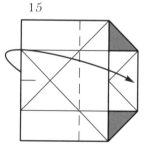

15. Fold the edge to the right, following the existing fold.

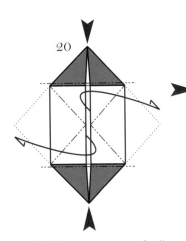

20

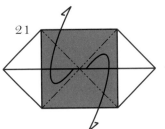

21

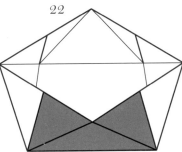

22

20. Through a series of valley folds open the box and immediately return to flatten it, bringing together the central points of the white layer where indicated by dotted lines. The operation will be easier if you push the upper and lower corners toward the inside.

21. At this point, shape the box by redoing the previous maneuver, but stop when the box goes into 3D. Then push gently on the right and left corners and open the central part at the same time. Stop when the box has assumed the desired shape.

22. The box is complete.

Box

Max Hulme

Take extra care to ensure all creases are accurate, or you may struggle!

1

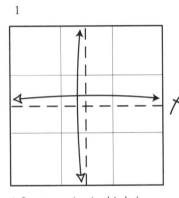

1. Start creasing in thirds (a method is shown under the techniques section). Crease in half and unfold in both directions.

2

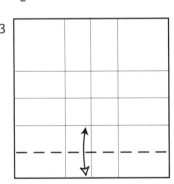

2. Fold an edge to the quarter crease, then unfold. Repeat 3 times.

3

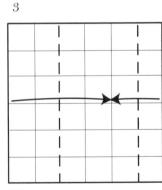

3. Fold so the left and right edges meet.

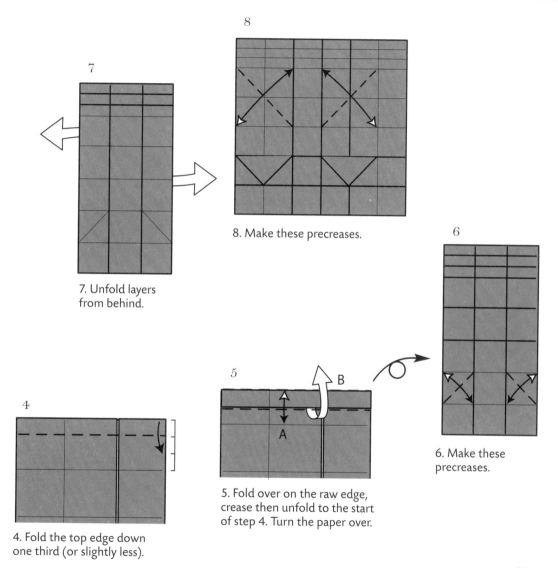

7. Unfold layers from behind.

8. Make these precreases.

6. Make these precreases.

5. Fold over on the raw edge, crease then unfold to the start of step 4. Turn the paper over.

4. Fold the top edge down one third (or slightly less).

39

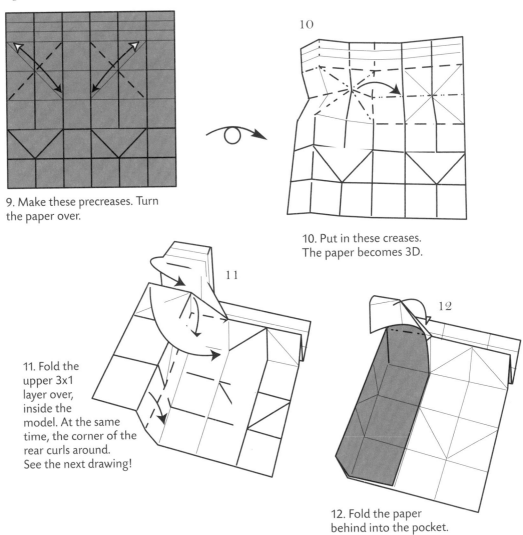

9

9. Make these precreases. Turn the paper over.

10

10. Put in these creases. The paper becomes 3D.

11

11. Fold the upper 3x1 layer over, inside the model. At the same time, the corner of the rear curls around. See the next drawing!

12

12. Fold the paper behind into the pocket.

40

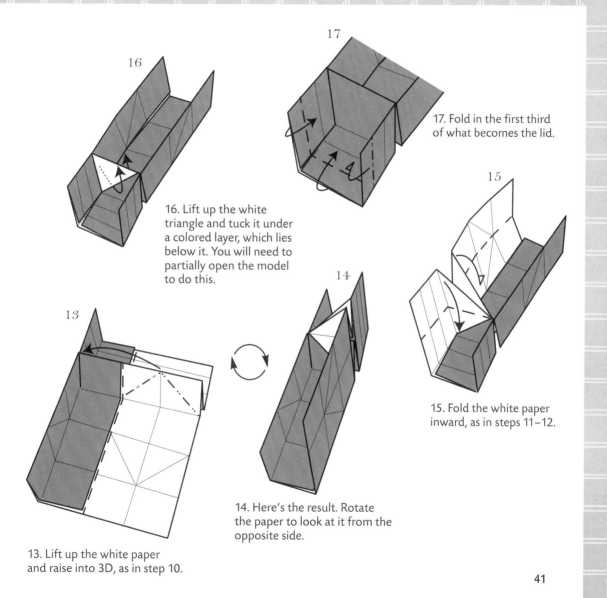

16. Lift up the white triangle and tuck it under a colored layer, which lies below it. You will need to partially open the model to do this.

17. Fold in the first third of what becomes the lid.

15. Fold the white paper inward, as in steps 11–12.

14. Here's the result. Rotate the paper to look at it from the opposite side.

13. Lift up the white paper and raise into 3D, as in step 10.

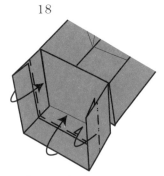

18

18. Repeat the last step.

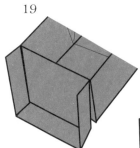

19

19. The lid is complete.

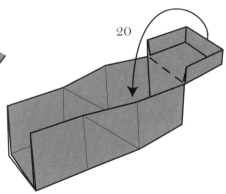

20

20. Fold the lid over so it lies between the layers.

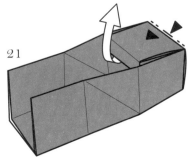

21

21. Reinforce the corner by pinching it (it's hard to do this later on!), then open the lid.

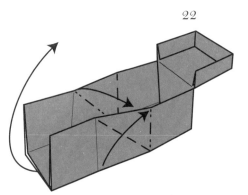

22

22. Swing the front end upward using these creases on either side.

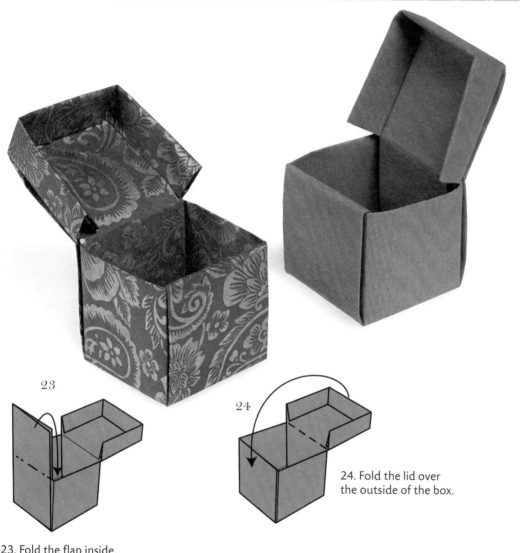

23

24

23. Fold the flap inside, creasing firmly to keep it in place.

24. Fold the lid over the outside of the box.

Fortune purse

Model by Francesco Mancini
Drawings by Francesco Decio and Francesco Mancini

The name of this little box derives from the fact that it reminded the designer of a change purse because of the two small triangles that fold to close it. It also reminded one of his friends of fortune cookies. This model is suitable for all kinds of paper, but works better if a little heavy.

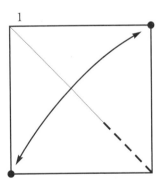

1. Fold and reopen to correspond with the dotted line.

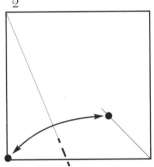

2. Fold and reopen to correspond with the dotted line.

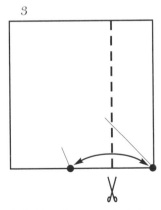

3. Fold and reopen. Cut along the dotted line.

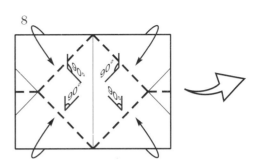

8. Lift the four edges.

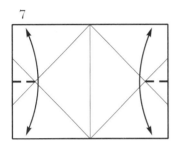

7. Fold and reopen to correspond with the dotted line.

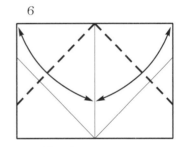

6. Fold and reopen.

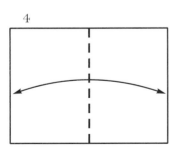

4. Fold and reopen.

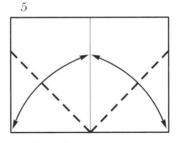

5. Fold and reopen.

45

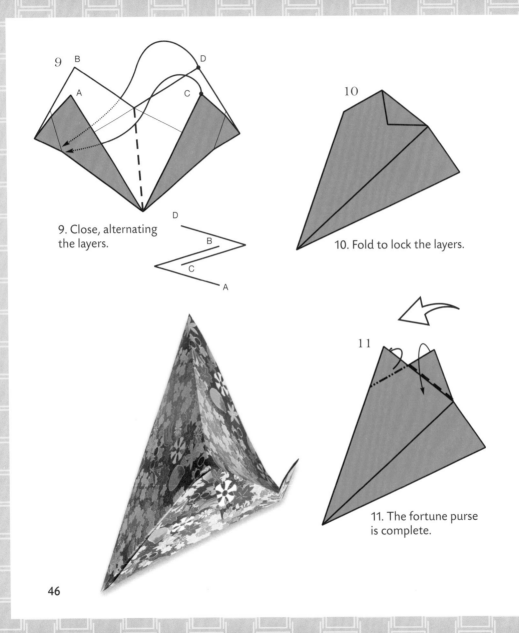

9. Close, alternating the layers.

10. Fold to lock the layers.

11. The fortune purse is complete.

Arianna's box

Riccardo Colletto

The author created this model, which folds quickly and easily, for the baptism of his daughter Arianna: it is an excellent way to quickly prepare a lot of favors for the most varied occasions. With the sheets provided you can get quite large boxes; if instead you want to use different paper, use a square sheet of at least 15–18 centimeters per side (6–7 inches).

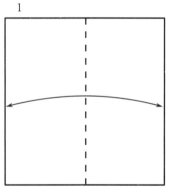

1. Fold in half and open again.

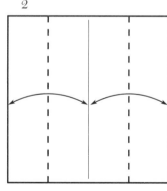

2. Fold in quarters and open again.

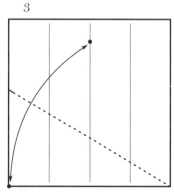

3. Pinch the paper on the edge, following the references.

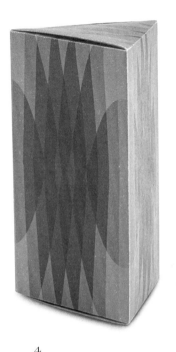

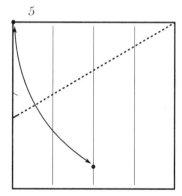

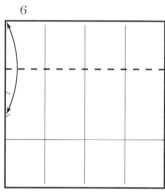

7. Rotate the model, bringing the two pinched marks upward.

6. Fold to the reference and reopen.

5. Pinch the paper on the edge, following the references.

4. Fold to the reference and reopen.

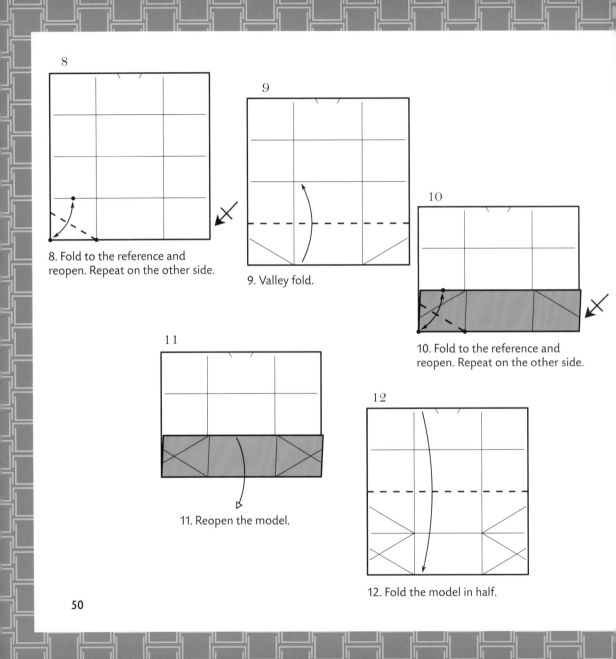

8

8. Fold to the reference and reopen. Repeat on the other side.

9

9. Valley fold.

10

10. Fold to the reference and reopen. Repeat on the other side.

11

11. Reopen the model.

12

12. Fold the model in half.

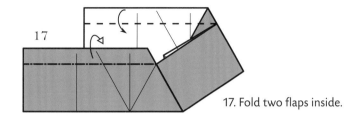

17. Fold two flaps inside.

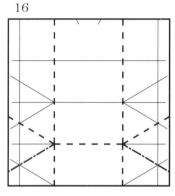

16. The model goes into 3D.

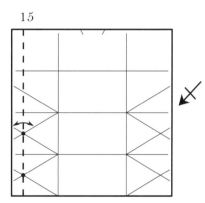

15. Fold along the references and reopen. Repeat on the other side.

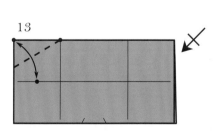

13. Fold to the reference and reopen. Repeat on the other side.

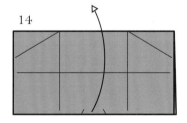

14. Reopen the model.

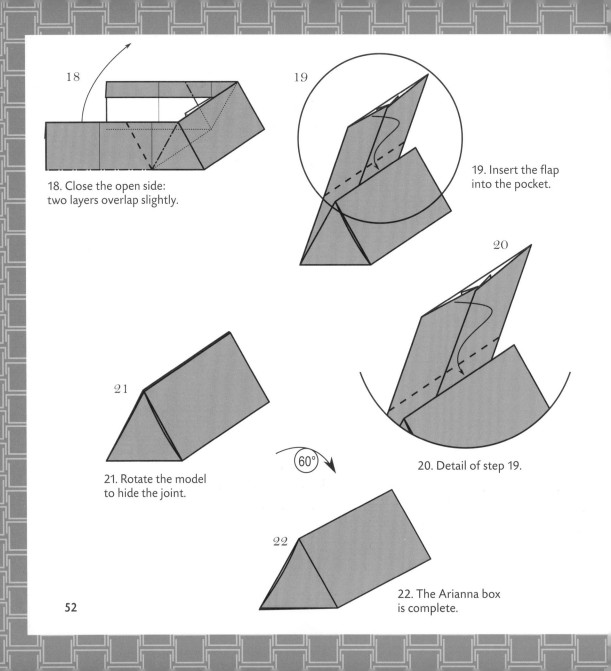

18. Close the open side:
two layers overlap slightly.

19. Insert the flap
into the pocket.

20. Detail of step 19.

60°

21. Rotate the model
to hide the joint.

22. The Arianna box
is complete.

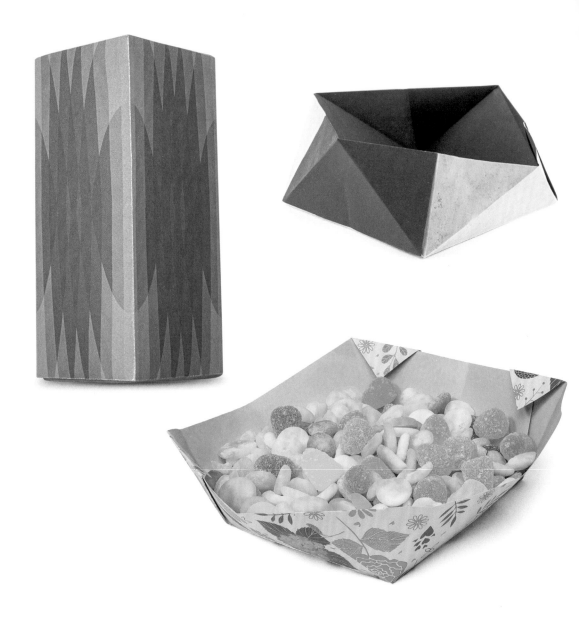